Self-Esteem

Workbook &

Journal.

*

101 Affirmations, Journal Questions and creative prompts.

Tony T Robinson

Author, Tony T Robinson

Title, Self-Esteem Workbook & Journal- 101 Affirmations, Journal Questions and creative prompts.

ISBN-13:978-1540802835

DEDICATION.

*

I would like to dedicate this book to my friends and family who have supported and inspired me throughout the creative process.

I would also like to dedicate this book to everyone who is on a journey trying to improve their self-esteem thereby improving the quality of their lives.

*

Also by

Tony T Robinson.

*

The Happiness Journal.

*

My 365 Day Guided Journal.

*

101 Journal questions for women.

*

101 Self Discovery Journal Prompts.

*

101 Quick and Easy Confidence Quotes.

*

101 Confidence Quotes that will change your life.

*

101 "I AM" Power Affirmations.

*

This Affirmation Workbook & Journal belongs to

Add your

Photo here.

Introduction.

*

Firstly let me congratulate and thank you for purchasing this workbook because it means that you are committed to making positive changes in your life and you are ready to become the best version of yourself that you can be which will make you stronger and more empowered, and for that you should pat yourself on the back.

My greatest hope is that this workbook will become your companion and confidant, and you use the journal pages to write and explore your feelings allowing the affirmations to change your life while having fun with the creative prompts.

I believe this workbook will benefit anyone who is committed to changing their life regardless of their sex, age, race or background. I also think it makes a perfect gift for anyone who may need to boost their self-esteem especially teenagers and young men & women but it is also great for mums dads, aunts & uncles, grandparents and teachers.

I personally wrote all of the affirmations in this book and have practiced many of them myself, so I know from personal and practical experience that they do work and I hope you enjoy incorporating them into your life as much as I have. I am a massive advocate of affirmations because I know how effective they can be. Using affirmations has helped me greatly in my life and I know they will benefit you to.

By writing and rewriting these affirmations you are taking responsibility and doing something positive to improve the quality of your life. You are not just sitting at home feeling sorry for yourself expecting things to miraculously change without putting in any effort. You are being proactive and taking charge of your life and by doing that you are saying to the universe -

"I am a powerful man/woman who is in control of my destiny and I am prepared to do whatever it takes to enhance my life". That in itself is an achievement because there are many people who are not prepared to change because they have become comfortable being unhappy.

I am glad you are not one of those people.

The Power of Affirmations.

*

Affirmations are an extremely powerful tool for change because they connect and speak directly to your unconscious which is the home of your internal programming.

Affirmations are like the code used in a computer. You will not be able to feel happy and positive if your programming is negative and undermining. Every time you think or say something like "I'm not good enough" "I will never be able to do that", "I'm so fat and ugly" you are reinforcing negative programming.

Now this may not be your fault. You may have been raised in a family who called you names or put you down and generally made you feel insecure and bad about yourself. They may not have even intended to do that, but if that was their programming then they would not have known how to behave in any other way and they certainly wouldn't have known how to install and instil self-esteem in you.

Your parents and your early environment create your first set of codes known as self-beliefs. These self-beliefs will inform and determine how you think and feel about yourself growing up and they will certainly determine future relationships, so unless any negative programming is identified and changed early on it will be carried through into adulthood and maybe even passed on to your children.

If your early programming is the only set of beliefs you have ever had it may be unsettling to think about changing them, or it may feel like an impossible task because they have been a part of you for such a long time which is perfectly understandable. Just have a little faith in yourself and the process; after all you have nothing to lose and everything to gain and I am living proof that affirmations work.

Affirmations are the best way to wipe the disc clean and rewrite your programming with new positive codes that are nurturing and supportive and here's how.

Every time you say something negative or destructive about yourself you need to use a positive affirmation to counteract and combat it. In order to change those thoughts you need to repeat the positive affirmation for at least one minute as this will help to reinstall some positivity back into your thinking. If you do this often enough eventually you will overwrite the negative thoughts and your auto response will sound like the new you with an abundance of healthy self-esteem.

Practicing affirmations on a daily basis will help to rewrite your programming at a core level which will have significant results in the way you think and feel about yourself. You may not even notice it at first but gradually you will see that you start to say nicer things about yourself and other people. You will wake up every morning feeling positive and good about yourself and your place in the world. You will feel that you are capable of doing anything and will start to look forward to greater challenges and eager to try new things rather than running away or trying to avoid them. It will also help to reduce anxiety and feelings of depression.

Think of affirmations as muscles. You can't go to the gym once, work out and by the time you get home you are toned in all the right places. It takes practice and repetition but the more you work out the greater the results will be. By using this workbook every day you are building your self-esteem muscles, and the bigger and stronger those muscles become the better you will feel about yourself and the more you will want to practice them.

The Power of Journaling.

*

Journaling is a wonderful way to understand and explore your feelings. It is an opportunity to purge and vent anger and negativity in a safe contained way. It can also be used to note and record all of the amazing things that happen in your life on a daily basis as well as the things that hurt or upset you.

You can use a journal to see how you have developed and grown as a person. It can help you to understand what you really want in life and how you can go about achieving those goals. When you write things down it will help you to be clear and specific about what you want rather than those ideas never developing from anything other than a passing thought.

When you journal you can really clarify and understand who you are as a person because you can learn about yourself in a completely different way. For example, if I asked the following question, "Who are you and what do you stand for" you would probably have to stop and think for a while in order to give a considered answer, I know I would, but having explored that question in a journal can really help you to define or redefine your perception of yourself and who you want to be in a way that you may not be able to easily verbalise. You may also find that when you journal you admit to things that you would never say out loud or to anyone else, so in that sense a journal can be like a best friend and very in-expensive therapist.

For me writing in a journal is a cathartic experience and it is helpful to imagine or visualise any negative painful feelings that you write down are flowing out of your body through the pen and onto the page where they are now trapped forever. They no longer belong to you; they have been released and gotten rid of.

This can feel like a cleansing and releasing experience which is an important part any healing process.

*

About this Workbook.

There are plenty of self-esteem and affirmations books, there are also books with random journal prompts and more recently art therapy colouring books, you may even come across a workbook or two but I have yet to find anything that encompasses and incorporates all of these elements in one place.

All of these tools can be very therapeutic in their own right but used together they are extremely potent which is why I have included affirmations to build your self-esteem, suggestions as how to be creative when practicing them, and corresponding journal prompts and questions that relate to each affirmation.

The question or prompt may require you to explore how you feel about the affirmation or how it relates to you and your life. It may ask you to create a list or describe a previous experience. (Please note, these are only suggestions and you can write about anything you want, it is your journal after all) There are a few blank spaces for you just to write whatever you feel without a prompt from me.

I have suggested creative ways in which you can write or decorate the affirmations and the pages. You can also be creative with the journal page if you want. Once again these are only suggestions and you can do whatever you want with the workbook and be as creative and colourful as you want to be.

Creativity has been proven to reduce anxiety and stress and can help combat the feelings of depression, so this book really has something to benefit everyone. Once you have completed your affirmation and journal page and decorated it in some way you will have something physical that you can look at and be proud of. This process will additionally boost your self-esteem in an enjoyable way.

Some of the affirmations and journal questions may require you to dig deep and possibly confront painful issues in your life. By confronting these issues and writing about them you can start to work through what holds you back and limits your ability to enjoy the life you not only want but deserve.

The journal pages are a great opportunity to purge negative feelings, and once you have released them you can finally be free of their power. If specific journal entries make you feel sad or upset that's ok because it means something is still unresolved and needs to be worked through. As you write about them imagine those feelings are now trapped on the page where they can no longer affect you. You can start to feel cleansed and purified of things that you would prefer not to have in your life. Once you have completed the journal entry I would recommend repeating the affirmation again so that you can return to a more positive state of mind.

If you are new to journaling then this is a wonderful way to begin exploring your thoughts and your feelings. Each affirmation and journal question has its own page but you can continue your thoughts on a note pad and then add the additional pages into the workbook. (You could attach or stick an envelope to each page as required and then keep your journal entries inside it so that they remain safe. If you prefer to type your journal answers you can certainly do that and then attach them to the appropriate page.

*

How to use this workbook.

*

I have incorporated both affirmations and journal questions so that one expands upon the other. This will not only help to boost your self-esteem but it will also release negative feelings and emotions and help you to try and understand where they come from and why they are affecting you.

You can either start at the beginning of the workbook and work your way through it day at a time repeating and rewriting each affirmation and completing the corresponding journal entry or, you can flick through the workbook and find the affirmation that best suits your needs on that day.

Whichever way you use the workbook is completely up to you. The important thing is that you use it regularly because the more you work the affirmations the more they will work for you.

Facebook Group.

Additionally and just for fun I have I created a specific Facebook group called "Affirmations journals and art therapy" Once you have completed a page you can take a photograph of it and upload it to the group to help and inspire the rest of the world. By sharing your work you are helping to create a community of people who are committed to improving their lives as well as the lives of others and I think that is truly special.

Also the more you share your work in the group the better you will feel about yourself and you will develop a greater sense of achievement which will increase your self-esteem and confidence. (Please don't post your journal entries as they are private and only for you)

In order to get the most from each affirmation I suggest repeating it 10 times either out loud or in your head before you write it down, then repeat it again or say it out loud a further 10 times before writing it again. Keep repeating this process until you have filled the entire page.

Repetition is the key. The more you practice something the better you become at it and using affirmations is no different. Repeating something once or twice isn't really going to have a significant or long lasting effect but the more you repeat them the more they will change your internal hardwiring and inner programming.

Also, just because you have completed a particular page once doesn't mean that you can't do it again. Take another piece of paper and rewrite and decorate the affirmation. In fact you can do this as many times as you want whether it be on one occasion or several weeks or months later.

I have lined some pages and purposefully left others blank so that you can either draw your own lines or find another way to write the affirmation. You may write them overlapping or in different colours in different directions. Let your imagination run free and just go with the flow.

Some of the affirmations have blank spaces that require you to complete and personalise them. I believe these are very powerful because what you choose to write is specific to you and will come from the heart so they will be more compelling as they relate specifically to you and your life. This also means that nobody else will have the exact same affirmation as you and that should make the experience more personal and enjoyable. `

Be Creative.

As I have mentioned before I want you to tap into your inner creativity which if you are already "arty" means you are probably rubbing your hands and colouring pencils together with glee, but if not don't worry because you don't have to be a qualified artist as this is just for fun, but you never know you might unleash hidden talents.

Just in case you need a bit of inspiration I have listed a few ideas that you might find useful and fun.

- Draw lines to write your affirmations on in different colours.
- Try using wavy lines or draw the lines at different angles going in different directions.
- Write the actual affirmation using different colours or different pens.
- Colour in the backgrounds behind individual lines or words or borders.
- Glue, tape or staple an envelope to the specific workbook page when you have additional journal sheets so that they don't get lost. You can also use pretty envelopes, make your own or decorate an old envelope.
- Use different fonts or writing styles.
- Decorate your pages with doodles and drawings either in black and white or with colour.
- Write the affirmations in different directions on the page.
- Use calligraphy.
- Let your affirmations overlap.
- Include pictures or photographs as they can be powerful visual reminders.
- Add stickers.
- Draw patterned borders on your page then colour them in.
- Write the affirmations in boxes and colour them in.
- Zentangle the affirmation or page in some way.
- Cut a pattern around the edge of a page or use a hole punch.

- (I would NOT recommend using felt tip pens or markers as they may bleed through the page)
- Why not take a picture of yourself either holding the book or open at a page you have worked on and post that in the facebook group.

If you still feel like you need some extra visual inspiration you can visit my Pintrest board called "Decorate Your Journal" where I have pinned lots of ideas that I thought you might enjoy. Some of them look quite professional so don't worry if you are not at that standard. *(You can find the link on my website **Transform Your Life with Tony T Robinson** under the heading My Books)which will contain the Pintrest link.*

*

Before you begin.

*

Just a quick reminder.

I want this workbook to be a useful tool that helps you to build your self-esteem but I also want it to be fun and enjoyable.

The creative and journal prompts are there only as a guideline, remember this is your journal so please feel free to write about whatever you want, and I hope that you join the Facebook group "Affirmations Journals art therapy & poetry" to share your creations with the rest of the world.

When practicing the affirmations, I would suggest saying each one either out loud or in your head 10 times before writing it down. Then say it again a further 10 times before writing it down on the next line, repeat this process until the page is complete. This way you are giving the affirmation the best chance to work its magic.

*

You can also find my YouTube channel by searching for **Transform your life with Tony T.**

On my channel there are affirmation and motivational videos to help you boost your confidence and self-esteem.

Self-esteem Declaration.

I wrote this self-esteem declaration to help motivate and inspire people. Please feel free to write your own incorporating everything that is important to you. Then make sure that you read it daily.

I am a STRONG and **CONFIDENT** person who is **capable** of doing anything I set my mind to because I have complete FAITH in myself and my abilities. I am strong enough to face all of life's hurdles because I know they are sent to make me a **stronger** better person. I believe that every situation is an opportunity to learn something new about myself and to grow into my full potential. Sometimes life can be tough but I know that *I AM TOUGHER*. Every day I do something to achieve my goals because *I am a unique and special person* who is deserving of every good thing the universe has to offer and in return I offer myself to be of service to others. I am **GRATEFUL** for all that I have and for all that I am yet to receive. I am thankful for everything that has ever happened to me and for all that the future will bestow upon me. I know this is exactly where I am supposed to be at this very moment in time because the Universe is preparing me for where I need to go and for what I need to do. Every day is an opportunity to *LIVE, LOVE and LAUGH* and to revel in the beauty of the world around me. I am connected to myself in the deepest of ways and I love and appreciate myself 100%. I am committed to making my life better so that I can help others to do the same. I know that LOVE is all around me and I live with a **PURE HEART** and good intentions. I breathe **POSITIVITY and HOPE** and I know that I can change the world around me by changing the world inside of me. I live to be inspired and to inspire others and I know that my words and actions have power and I am RESPONSIBLE for everything that happens in my life. *I am MOTIVATED* to make choices that are right for my MIND BODY and SPIRIT and I am able to create the life I want for myself with every thought and every action. I know that my personal power comes from my belief in myself and my desire to develop and grow. I start my day with a still mind, a **kind heart** and a positive attitude. I believe that I am a valuable person who has much to offer the world so today I will be the BEST that I can be and do the BEST that I can do in every situation. *I LOVE MYSELF* for my achievements and I forgive myself for past mistakes because they will teach me how to succeed in the future. I refuse to allow negativity into my life and I will remain STRONG and POSITIVE through the good times and the bad. I am a **CONFIDENCE WARRIOR** who is determined to live up to my unlimited potential. *I LOVE, HONOUR and CHERISH* myself, my friends and my family and I am committed to making today and every day absolutely **AMAZING.**

By Tony T Robinson.

25

Affirmation # 1

(Complete this affirmation in a few sentences and glue a photograph of yourself on the page in order to celebrate and embrace yourself and the work you are doing to develop and improve your self-esteem. Draw a border around the photograph using different shapes, patterns and colours)

My name is _____

and_____

_____

_____

_____

Journal Question.

Who are you? This is a great opportunity to expand and elaborate on your affirmation and create a positive definition of you are or who you would like to be.

I am

Affirmation # 2

(Repeat and rewrite the affirmation until the entire page is full.
Use different coloured pens)

"I am a powerful person and I am in charge of my life and my destiny"

....

....

....

....

....

....

....

....

....

....

....

....

....

Journal Question.

How do you feel after repeating this affirmation? In what ways do you feel in charge of your life?

_____

_____

_____

_____

_____

_____

_____

_____

_____

_____

_____

_____

_____

_____

_____

_____

_____

Remember you are Awesome!

Affirmation # 3

(Repeat and complete this affirmation adding as many things as you can) Thought – use different colour pens.

Today I am truly Grateful for

_____

_____

_____

_____

_____

_____

_____

_____

_____

_____

_____

_____

_____

_____

_____

_____

_____

Journal Question.

Explore in greater detail what you are most grateful for and why. How do you express and show your gratitude? Perhaps showing gratitude is something you need to improve and do more often.

****

****

****

****

****

****

****

****

****

****

****

****

****

****

****

****

Affirmation # 4

(Repeat 10 times before writing the affirmation. Do this every time until the page is complete. Draw a spiral border around the page and colour it in)

"I LOVE and ACCEPT myself for who I am this very moment and I am a man / woman of Beauty Strength and Courage"

Journal Entry.

Explore your thoughts and feelings in relation to this affirmation. I know it may be hard, if so then explore why it's hard. **(make a commitment to repeat it every day until you believe it)**

Affirmation # 5

(Write the words Love Wealth Happiness in different colours and different sizes)

This is a great affirmation to incorporate visualisation. Imagine yourself standing with your arms open wide to the universe and love wealth and happiness are streams of different coloured light that you are drawing into your life and that are filling you up.

"I attract an abundance of Love Wealth and Happiness into my life"

Journal entry.

This affirmation is important to me because_____

Affirmation # 6

"Today I am surrounded by Positive Healing Energy"

(Write this affirmation in large letters and then use different coloured pencils to draw what you think that healing energy would look like. While you are doing this keep repeating the affirmation)

Journal entry.

What area of your life requires the most healing and why? How will healing that thing change or affect your life?

_____

_____

_____

_____

_____

_____

_____

_____

_____

_____

_____

_____

_____

_____

_____

_____

_____

_____

_____

_____

_____

Affirmation # 7

(Use different colours to draw the lines to write on. Repeat 10 times before writing out the affirmation)

"I promise I will never give away my personal power or let people treat me badly"

Journal entry.

Explore in what ways you have given away your personal power or allowed someone to treat you badly. What have you learned from that situation?

Affirmation # 8

(Repeat and complete this affirmation rewriting it until the page is full)

My greatest goal in life is -

Journal entry.

Why is this goal important to you?

_____

_____

_____

_____

_____

_____

_____

_____

_____

_____

_____

_____

_____

_____

_____

_____

_____

_____

_____

_____

You can achieve anything because you are amazing.

Affirmation # 9

(Be creative in how you use this affirmation, Include lots of colours and shapes. make sure you repeat it out loud for at least one minute)

"I am Strong and fearless"

Journal entry.

Write about ways in which you are strong, either now or in the past and list times & situations when you were FEARLESS or overcame something that was difficult for you.

Affirmation # 10

(Repeat at least 10 times before writing it) Idea – instead of dotting the letter I as you would normally, draw a red heart in its place to represent love and forgiveness. You can also use hearts to decorate the page)

"I Forgive myself for bringing my past into the present and I let go of all pain and sorrow"

Journal entry.

In what ways have you allowed your past to affect your future?
What pain and sorrow do you need to let go of?

_____

_____

_____

_____

_____

_____

_____

_____

_____

_____

_____

_____

_____

_____

_____

_____

_____

**Don't punish yourself for previous actions instead know that
you can now make positive choices now.**

Affirmation # 11

"I am not just a Daughter, a Wife, A Mother, a Lover, or friend I am an independent valuable woman in my own right"

(Repeat this affirmation 10 times before writing it) Perhaps you could include a photograph of you at different times of your life when you felt strong and independent. (Men, you can replace the female to male)

Journal entry.

Do you feel that you have become just a *title* and not your own person? Have you lost who you really are? If so reclaim your individuality here by writing how you intend to reclaim that independence in your daily life.

Affirmation # 12

(Write each sentence in a different colour pen in different sizes in different directions. Don't worry if they overlap or if it looks messy. Let go and get crazy.)

"Every day I believe in myself more and more"

Journal entry.

In what ways do you believe in yourself and is there an area of your life where you need more self-belief?

_____

_____

_____

_____

_____

_____

_____

_____

_____

_____

_____

_____

_____

_____

_____

_____

_____

_____

_____

_____

_____

Never forget what a wonderful person you are.

Affirmation # 13

(Repeat the affirmation 10 times before writing it out) Write the words in capital letters in different colours. Maybe alternate the colours on each line)

"I am FUN, FABULOUS and FRIENDLY and I LOVE myself"

Journal entry.

In what ways does this affirmation describe you?

_____
_____
_____
_____
_____
_____
_____
_____
_____
_____
_____
_____
_____
_____
_____
_____
_____
_____
_____

Affirmation # 14

(Rip up different pieces of coloured paper and stick them on the page then repeat the affirmation 10 times every time you write it out)

"I am a truly unique person and I celebrate my Individuality"

Journal entry.

Make a list of all your wonderful unique qualities and attributes.

_____

_____

_____

_____

_____

_____

_____

_____

_____

_____

_____

_____

_____

_____

_____

_____

_____

_____

_____

_____

Never forget.......... You are Fierce & Fabulous.

Affirmation # 15

(Make a list of as many things as you can)

I am a good person because _____

_____

_____

_____

_____

_____

_____

_____

_____

_____

_____

_____

_____

_____

_____

_____

_____

_____

_____

Journal entry.

Expand upon the affirmation.

Affirmation # 16

(Write this affirmation as many times as you can)

"I love and accept my flaws because they are a part of who I am"

Journal Question.

We all have flaws that we usually criticise or berate ourselves for, instead list those flaws and explore ways to love and accept them because they are a part of who you are. Self-acceptance is the foundation of self-esteem.

_____

_____

_____

_____

_____

_____

_____

_____

_____

_____

_____

_____

_____

_____

_____

_____

_____

_____

_____

_____

_____

Affirmation # 17

(Draw several boxes to write the affirmation in, then add colour and pattern either in or around the box, or both)

"I am Grateful for my ability to make a difference in the World"

Journal entry.

Explore or write a list of ways in which you make a difference in the world and before you say you don't, you do and you can make a difference. – Keep positive. If this is a really tough one for you ask a friend or family member. They will be able to see your special qualities even if you cannot.

Affirmation # 18

(Draw lots of hearts and colour them in, once you have done that write the affirmation in/through/over/around them)

"I am Sensitive & Caring and I love that about myself"

Journal entry.

Sometimes people can be accused of being overly sensitive and that is used against them. Remind yourself of why being sensitive and caring makes you a good person.

I like being Sensitive and caring because

Affirmation # 19

"I let go of all anxiety and worry. They no longer belong to me. Instead I am Confident in my Capabilities"

(While writing this affirmation let go of any restrictions and just be creative)

Journal Question.

What are your main anxieties and explore where they came from, also think about areas in which you are confident and capable and have overcome those anxieties. *(continue on another sheet of paper if you need to and stick it in)*

_____

_____

_____

_____

_____

_____

_____

_____

_____

_____

_____

_____

_____

_____

_____

_____

_____

_____

You are stronger than you think you are!

Affirmation # 20

(Repeat the affirmation out loud 10 times before writing it down)
Idea – you could include pictures of what the affirmations represents to you.

"My soul is open to all the beauty that surrounds me and is within me"

Journal entry.

Affirmation # 21

(Write this affirmation in calming colours or perhaps a different style of handwriting, one that is freer and flows more)

"I am Calm and Relaxed and all is well in my world"

Journal entry.

For many people staying calm and relaxed is a difficult task. So explore ways in which you can remain calm or think about the things that stress you out so that you can prepare for them in the future and then keep this affirmation in mind.

Affirmation # 22

(Write this one as many times as you can on the page. maybe draw different coloured lines or use different coloured pens. Colour in the whole page before writing the affirmation)

"I AM WORTHY"

Journal Question.

How does saying this affirmation make you feel? Is this a difficult one for you, if so why? *Thought – Just because other people are negative or treat you badly and put you down, that doesn't mean that they are right. It only means they don't feel worthy and this is their way of dealing with it and expressing it.*

Don't forget to write down reasons why you are worthy.

Affirmation # 23

(Keep adding to the list and when completed repeat several times)

I am Stronger than my Pain.

I am Stronger than my Tears.

I am Stronger than my Anxiety.

I am Stronger than my Fear.

I am stronger than _____

I am stronger than _____

I am stronger than _____

I am stronger than _____

I am stronger than _____

I am stronger than _____

I am stronger than _____

I am stronger than _____

I am stronger than _____

I am stronger than _____

I am stronger than _____

I am stronger than _____

I am stronger than _____

Journal Question.

Did you realise just how strong you were?

Affirmation # 24

(Repeat 10 times before rewriting the affirmation)

"I allow myself to fully connect to my feelings. When I feel sad or need to cry I know that it is ok because it's healing and helps me to release my emotions"

Journal entry

I feel

....

....

....

....

....

....

....

....

....

....

....

....

....

....

....

....

Affirmation # 25

(Write this affirmation vertically and diagonally and let them cross over. Keep repeating the affirmation while you are writing it)

"My thoughts are Positive and Powerful and I am in charge of MY life"

Journal entry.

Make a list or write down what positive and powerful thoughts you have or that inspire you.

Affirmation # 26

(Fill in the blanks and then randomly write those words all over the page.

"I am worthy of Happiness _____, _____ and _____ "

Journal entry.

I am WORTHY because

Just remember how great you are because you deserve the best of everything.

Affirmation # 27

(Write this affirmation in a chain around the page, not in straight lines)

"I know that I am liked because I am a good person"

Journal Question.

Quite often repeating positive affirmations are met with internal resistance and an internal negative voice that wants to challenge what you are saying because it is new or alien. So explore what you felt while writing this affirmation and what your internal resistance sounded like. Once you have completed your journal entry repeat the affirmation again.

You are a good person. I know it and other people know it.
Now you need to know it.

Affirmation # 28

(Write this affirmation in a different style of handwriting. See how many different ways you can write it)

"I am Happy and Confident in all social

situations and I enjoy meeting new people"

Journal entry.

If you feel anxious in social situations explore why you feel that way and what is it you believe other people are thinking about you.

Affirmation # 29

(Complete the affirmation and then keep copying it out until the page is full. You can use a different word each time you write it out)

"As I write these words I release my inner Courage and Confidence and I step into the _____ person I was destined to be"

_____

_____

_____

_____

_____

_____

_____

_____

_____

_____

_____

_____

_____

_____

_____

_____

_____

Journal Question.

Think about a situation that caused you anxiety, but you pushed through it anyway. Write down how you felt before and after?

_____

_____

_____

_____

_____

_____

_____

_____

_____

_____

_____

_____

_____

_____

_____

_____

_____

_____

_____

_____

Affirmation # 30

(Complete the list and then read it at least ten times)

I decide what is good for me.

I decide what is right for me.

I decide what makes me happy.

I decide who makes me happy

I decide what I can do.

I decide _____

I decide _____

I decide _____

I decide _____

I decide _____

I decide _____

I decide _____

I decide _____

I decide _____

I decide _____

I decide _____

I decide _____

I decide _____

Journal entry.

Never forget that you are responsible for the decisions you make in your life and that makes you a very powerful person. Explore that thought.

Affirmation # 31

(Complete the affirmation and keep writing it)

My Health is important to me so today I am going to -

_____

_____

_____

_____

_____

_____

_____

_____

_____

_____

_____

_____

_____

_____

_____

_____

_____

_____

_____

_____

_____

_____

_____

Journal Question.

What other things can you start doing to improve your health?
Remember that small daily changes can accumulate into massive
results. No marathon is run in one step.

Affirmation # 32

(JUST FOR EXTRA EMPHASIS WRITE THIS AFFIRMATION IN CAPITAL LETTERS ALL ACROSS THE PAGE)

"I AM BOLD BEAUTIFUL AND BRAVE"

Journal Question.

I am BOLD, BEAUTIFUL, BRAVE and_____

_____

_____

_____

_____

_____

_____

_____

_____

_____

_____

_____

YOU ARE A WARRIOR. NEVER HOLD YOURSELF BACK.

Affirmation # 33

"Today I embrace my INNER DIVA and accept the power that emanates and radiates from deep within me"

(See how many times you can write INNER DIVA on the page)

Journal entry.

Being a Diva doesn't have to be negative. A Diva is a person who is strong and powerful and refuses to be treated badly. In this entry explore your Inner Diva.

Don't forget. You are FIERCE so don't let anybody take you for a fool.

Affirmation # 34

(Repeat this affirmation 10 times before writing it out)

"I let go of all Pain, Anger and Resentment and replace them with HAPPINESS, JOY and LOVE."

Journal Question.

I feel my self-esteem

Affirmation # 35

(Complete and repeat the affirmation)

I feel totally empowered when I

,,

,,

,,

,,

,,

,,

,,

,,

,,

,,

,,

,,

,,

,,

,,

,,

,,

,,

,,

,,

Journal Question.

What makes you feel empowered?

Affirmation # 36

"I recognise and realise that I deserve to be treated with Love and Respect by myself and by others"

Journal Question.

It can be very hard to expect or accept love and respect from other people when you don't feel that way about yourself in the first place. So has your ability to love and respect yourself grown since starting this journal?

How do you demonstrate to others that you love and respect yourself?

Affirmation # 37

(Draw and colour in a funky border around the page)

"I have the Power within me to overcome any and all adversity"

Journal Question.

What difficult times have you gotten through? Remind yourself that you are not only a survivor but you are a warrior.

_____

_____

_____

_____

_____

_____

_____

_____

_____

_____

_____

_____

_____

_____

_____

_____

_____

_____

You are one tough cookie. Stand up straight and hold your head high.

Affirmation # 38

(Write the word Negativity in a dark colour and Positivity in a bright colour.)

"Today I refuse to allow Negativity into my life because I am a Powerhouse of Positivity"

_____

_____

_____

_____

_____

_____

_____

_____

_____

_____

_____

_____

_____

_____

_____

_____

_____

_____

_____

_____

_____

_____

_____

_____

Journal entry.

Today I refuse to allow

Affirmation # 39

(Complete and repeat the affirmation) Then use different colours to fill in the letters.

I am a true gift to the world because_____

Journal entry.

Expand on the affirmation and write why you are a gift to the world.

Affirmation # 40

(Instead of writing the word love, draw a heart on every line) Idea - draw some clouds and sky at the bottom of the page)

"My self-esteem is sky high today and I love myself"

Journal Question.

In what ways do you feel your self-esteem has improved?

Affirmation # 41

(Randomly write out this affirmation using calming colours to decorate this page)

"I release all tension and anxiety from my body and all is well in my world"

Journal Question.

How do you feel after completing this affirmation?

Affirmation # 42

(Write the word BASK in big letters in the centre of the page and then write the affirmation from the centre point outwards all the way around the page. (like rays of light)

"Today I shall BASK in the beauty of who I am"

Journal Question.

What makes you beautiful or feel beautiful? (This page is for nice thoughts only)

_____

_____

_____

_____

_____

_____

_____

_____

_____

_____

_____

_____

_____

_____

_____

_____

_____

_____

_____

_____

_____

Never forget: You are beautiful inside and out.

Affirmation # 43

(See how many times you can write the word Beautiful on the page; try using different colours different fonts, different patterns, upside down etc, create a border or doodle around the words)

"I AM BEAUTIFUL"

Journal entry.

I am Beautiful because -

Affirmation # 44

"I refuse to be defined by other people's expectations and ideas of who I should be because I am my own person and I am Perfect just as I am"

Journal entry.

Do you feel that you have had to hide or supress who you really are to please other people, if so write a definition of who you really are or who you want to be.

_____

_____

_____

_____

_____

_____

_____

_____

_____

_____

_____

_____

_____

_____

_____

_____

_____

_____

_____

_____

_____

Affirmation # 45

(Write this in a square working your way in from the outside of the page to the centre)

"Every Day I wake up knowing that GOD is in my corner fighting for me"

Journal entry.

"Every day I wake up knowing that God is in my corner fighting for me and _____

_____

_____

_____

_____

_____

_____

_____

_____

_____

_____

_____

_____

_____

_____

_____

_____

_____

Affirmation # 46

(Repeat 10 times before writing the affirmation)

"I am stronger Today than I was Yesterday and Tomorrow I will be stronger than I am Today"

Journal Question.

What can you do on a daily basis to boost your self-esteem and confidence?

_____

_____

_____

_____

_____

_____

_____

_____

_____

_____

_____

_____

_____

_____

_____

_____

_____

_____

Affirmation # 47

(Write the word Gratitude as many times as you can on the page and use lots of colour while repeating the affirmation)

"I am overflowing with Gratitude for all that I have and all that I am yet to receive"

Journal entry.

Make a list of all the things or people that you are most grateful for.

Affirmation # 48

(Complete and rewrite this affirmation)

"I am STRONG and _____

"I am STRONG and _____

"I am STRONG and _____

"I am STRONG and _____

"I am STRONG and _____

"I am STRONG and _____

"I am STRONG and _____

"I am STRONG and _____

"I am STRONG and _____

"I am STRONG and _____

"I am STRONG and _____

"I am STRONG and _____

"I am STRONG and _____

"I am STRONG and _____

"I am STRONG and _____

"I am STRONG and _____

"I am STRONG and _____

Journal Entry.

Did you realise you were so strong. *Remember this in future.*

Affirmation # 49

(Write this big and bold over two lines rather than one and then when the page is full write it again starting on the second line so that you are writing over yourself)

"Fear will only hold me back if I let it but today I choose to be Brave & Fearless & I am in charge of my life"

Journal Question.

What fears have you allowed to hold you back and how has this affected your life?

_____

_____

_____

_____

_____

_____

_____

_____

_____

_____

_____

_____

_____

_____

_____

_____

_____

_____

_____

You are a Fearless Warrior and You can do anything.

Affirmation # 50

(Start by drawing wavy lines across the page then copy out the affirmation)

"I AM MOTIVATED TO GET THE BEST OUT OF TODAY AND I LIVE EVERY MOMENT TO THE FULLEST.

Journal Entry.

What is your motivation? How can you stay connected to the feeling?

_____

_____

_____

_____

_____

_____

_____

_____

_____

_____

_____

_____

_____

_____

_____

_____

_____

_____

Affirmation # 51

(Complete and repeat – you may have several things to let go of so you can make a list)

"I freely release and let go of

_____

_____

"I freely release and let go of

_____

_____

"I freely release and let go of

_____

_____

"I freely release and let go of

_____

_____

"I freely release and let go of

_____

_____

"I freely release and let go of

_____

_____

"I freely release and let go of

_____

_____

"I freely release and let go of

_____

_____

Journal entry.

Affirmation # 52

(Use a different coloured pencil to fill in each line to create a colourful background)

"I give up judging myself and replace those criticisms with caring and nurturing thoughts"

Journal Question.

In what ways, and why do you judge and criticise yourself? Make a promise to yourself to stop doing that and to only speak about yourself with words of love. Make a list of self-compliments.

Affirmation # 53

(On the blank lines write the affirmation in different colours or colour in the background.

"I no longer care what other people think of me. Instead I am focused on who I am and what is right for me"

_____

_____

_____

"I no longer care what other people think of me. Instead I am focused on who I am and what is right for me"

_____

_____

_____

"I no longer care what other people think of me. Instead I am focused on who I am and what is right for me"

_____

_____

_____

*

Journal Question.

What is your greatest fear in relation to how other people perceive you and why do you care what they think?

_____

_____

_____

_____

_____

_____

_____

_____

_____

_____

_____

_____

_____

_____

_____

_____

You are Perfect just as you are. Remember other people's opinions are just that - their opinions.

Affirmation # 54

(Complete and repeat the affirmation)

"I am responsible for Creating my Reality so I am going to _____

_____

_____

_____

_____

_____

_____

_____

_____

_____

_____

_____

_____

_____

_____

_____

_____

Journal entry.

How is this reality different to your current reality and what can you do to change that?

_____

_____

_____

_____

_____

_____

_____

_____

_____

_____

_____

_____

_____

_____

_____

_____

_____

_____

_____

_____

Affirmation # 55

(Copy out the affirmation anywhere on the page)

"Today I let go of negative habits and do what is best for my Mind Body and Spirit"

Journal Question.

What habits can you change and what positive healthy habits can you replace them with?

Affirmation # 56

I

am

my

own

best

friend

and

I

like

myself.

Journal Question.

What do you like the most about yourself?

Affirmation # 57

(Draw a heart instead or writing the word heart)

"I am a GOOD person I have a kind Heart and I like who I am"

Journal entry.

The things I like best about me are _____

_____

_____

_____

_____

_____

_____

_____

_____

_____

_____

_____

_____

_____

_____

_____

_____

_____

_____

_____

Affirmation # 58

(Write each alternative affirmation upside down in a different colour)

"I let go of all negativity and allow my Inner Light to Shine through"

Journal entry.

In what ways do you think you have changed for the better?

Affirmation # 59

(Continue writing out the affirmation starting each one with the next letter in the alphabet)

I am Amazing.

I am Beautiful.

I am Compassionate.

I am Determined.

I am _____

I am _____

I am _____

I am _____

I am _____

I am _____

I am _____

I am _____

I am _____

I am _____

I am _____

I am _____

I am _____

I am _____

Journal question.

How does it feel referring to yourself with so many positive words?

Affirmation # 60

(Imagine you are connected by a thin chord to the person in this affirmation and every time you repeat it and write it know that you are cutting that chord and setting yourself free)

"I offer Peace and Love to anyone who has ever hurt me so that they no longer take up space in my life"

Journal entry.

I know this is probably a difficult affirmation for you to repeat let alone believe. But holding on to pain and hurt from the past only keeps you attached to the person who hurt you. I am not suggesting that what they did was ok, and they never need to know that you have forgiven them because it is not about making them feel better. It is about making you feel better.

I feel -

Affirmation # 61

(Repeat for at least 1 minute and write the affirmation in smaller letters over the typed version in different colours)

"Tonight

I shall sleep deeply

and Peacefully and

tomorrow I will wake

up rejuvenated &

ready to have a

fantastic day"

Journal Question.

Describe your perfect day.

Affirmation # 62

(Repeat and rewrite)

I _____

Am _____

Too _____

BLESSED _____

To _____

Be _____

STRESSED _____

I _____

Am _____

Too _____

BLESSED _____

To _____

Be _____

STRESSED _____

Journal Question.

In what ways do you feel blessed?

Affirmation # 63

(Repeat this affirmation 20 times every time before you write it out) if you get to the end of the page and it still feels uncomfortable or difficult get another piece of paper and do it again)

"When I look in the mirror I see a beautiful woman/ hansom man who is capable of anything"

Journal entry.

Make a list of things you find beautiful about yourself. Let go of your critical eye and slide in a filter of love and compassion.

Affirmation # 64

(See how many times you can repeat the affirmation) Why not use different colours or fonts. Don't forget you can decorate the page in any way you want)

I love my face. I love my Body. I love me.

Journal Question.

This affirmation is a continuation from the one on the previous page, hopefully you found it easier to complete. Write about how you feel now saying this affirmation. Try to look for the positives.

Affirmation # 65

(Write the words I CAN DO IT as many times as you can on the page)
use different colours and writing styles, don't worry if you write over
yourself and just have fun. .

"Whatever situation I find myself in I will repeat
these words.

I

CAN

DO

IT!

Journal Question.

Whenever you feel nervous and scared, regardless of the situation remember this affirmation and keep repeating I CAN DO IT as it will help to get you through it.

What situations make you the most anxious and why?

Affirmation # 66

(Draw lots of boxes on the page then write the affirmation in each one, don't forget to use lots of colour)

"I let go of Yesterday. I live and breathe every moment of Today and I am prepared to do it again Tomorrow"

Journal Question.

Think about how you can live in the moment and be fully connected to the here and now rather than living in the past. If you are not connected to the present what might you be missing out on?

Affirmation # 67

(Repeat this affirmation as you write it nice and big)

"Today I will put MY NEEDS first and that is ok"

_____

_____

_____

_____

_____

_____

_____

_____

_____

_____

_____

_____

_____

_____

_____

_____

_____

Journal Question.

Does it feel difficult to put your needs first? Why? Which of your needs have you been neglecting but will now start to make a priority?

Affirmation # 68

I am motivated to be the best person I can be"

Journal entry.

Describe the best version of yourself. I am _____

Affirmation # 69

(Repeat repeat repeat)and use relaxing colours around the page.

"Every fibre of my being is CALM and RELAXED"

Journal Entry.

What things can you do to introduce more relaxation into your life.

Affirmation # 70

(Randomly write the words Love & Joy in different sizes anywhere on the page while repeating the affirmation)

"I attract an ABUNDANCE of LOVE & JOY into my life"

Journal Entry.

This affirmation makes me feel_____

_____

_____

_____

_____

_____

_____

_____

_____

_____

_____

_____

_____

_____

_____

_____

_____

_____

_____

_____

_____

_____

_____

_____

Affirmation # 71

"Today I freely release Guilt and Shame and make space for Love and Happiness"

Journal Entry.

Guilt and shame are powerful emotions and they can be very destructive so it is good to release them. I am sure this affirmation may cause a lot of feelings to rise to the surface so you can explore & release them here.

I _____

_____

_____

_____

_____

_____

_____

_____

_____

_____

_____

_____

_____

_____

_____

*

Affirmation # 72

(Write out a list)

Today I remove the things that no longer serve me and I replace them with_____

Journal entry.

(Once you have completed your journal entry repeat the affirmation again imagining that you are throwing all of those things out and you can feel the positive replacements coming in.

Affirmation # 73

"I am in control of what and when I eat, so today I will only eat when I am hungry and stop when I am full"

Journal entry.

If your diet or weight is an issue for you then repeating this affirmation can help in terms of managing cravings and to help prevent eating when you are not physically hungry.

What does this affirmation trigger anything in you?

Affirmation # 74

(Write this any way you want to)

"I release all Earthly Limitations and give Thanks & Praise to a power greater than my own"

Journal Question.

What limitations would you like to let go of?

Affirmation # 75

(Repeat at least ten times before writing each one out)

"Regardless of any anxiety I may feel, today I will push through it and prove to myself that I am capable of anything"

Journal Entry.

This affirmation makes me _____

_____

_____

_____

_____

_____

_____

_____

_____

_____

_____

_____

_____

_____

_____

_____

_____

_____

_____

_____

_____

Affirmation # 76

(Repeat and rewrite)

"I may not have everything I want but I have everything I need"

Journal Entry.

This affirmation makes me realise

_____

_____

_____

_____

_____

_____

_____

_____

_____

_____

_____

_____

_____

_____

_____

_____

_____

_____

_____

_____

_____

Never forget there is always someone with less than you.

Affirmation # 77

(Write a nice long list, and don't forget you can always come back and add more to the list)

I am defined by my Good Qualities which are –

_____

_____

_____

_____

_____

_____

_____

_____

_____

_____

_____

_____

_____

_____

_____

_____

Journal Question.

I feel great acknowledging my good qualities because _____

Affirmation # 78

(Make a list of your 10 favourite affirmations that you have already completed and then read that list 10 times)

Journal Question.

What do you notice about the affirmations you have chosen. Is there a common theme? Does it highlight a specific area that you need to work on?

Affirmation # 79

(You can complete this affirmation with one specific thing or a list, it's up to you)

I LET GO OF _____

Journal Entry.

Explore further what you would like to let go of and why?

Affirmation # 80

(You can either create a list or complete the affirmation in one sentence and then repeat it)

I Honour myself by _____

_____

_____

_____

_____

_____

_____

_____

_____

_____

_____

_____

_____

_____

_____

_____

_____

*

Journal Question.

What other ways can you honour yourself?

Affirmation # 81

(Repeat and Rewrite)

"I Promise that I will always carry myself with Dignity and Grace"

Journal Entry.

Are there situations where it is easy for someone to ruffle your feathers or where you quickly lose control? How can you maintain your composure and carry yourself with dignity and grace?

*

Affirmation # 82

(Try writing this affirmation as small as you can. Imagine it at a cellular level) colour in the background of each line.

"I am energised and full of life and I can feel my body healing itself at a cellular level"

Journal Question.

If you have any health concerns explore what they are here.

Affirmation # 83

(Repeat the affirmation 10 times and then write it in the spaces)

"I have complete Faith in Myself and my Abilities"

_____

"I have complete Faith in Myself and my Abilities"

_____

"I have complete Faith in Myself and my Abilities"

_____

"I have complete Faith in Myself and my Abilities"

_____

"I have complete Faith in Myself and my Abilities"

_____

"I have complete Faith in Myself and my Abilities"

_____

"I have complete Faith in Myself and my Abilities"

_____

"I have complete Faith in Myself and my Abilities"

_____

Journal Entry.

Explore what you think your abilities are.

Affirmation # 84

(Write this in a higgledy piggeldy way)

"Today I remove any anxiety negativity and pain from my life and I revel in the beauty of all that I am"

Journal entry.

Today I remove any anxiety, negativity and pain from my life and I relish in the beauty of all that Is and I am ....

Affirmation # 85

(You decide how to write this affirmation)

"Every day I Praise & Value myself for just being ME"

Journal entry.

Imagine you were someone else praising you, what would you say about yourself?

Affirmation # 86

(Repeat at least 10 times before writing the affirmation down)

"I forgive everyone who has ever hurt me because forgiveness cleanses and heals me"

_____

_____

_____

_____

_____

_____

_____

_____

_____

_____

_____

_____

_____

_____

_____

_____

_____

Journal entry.

I feel -

Affirmation # 87

(Write this affirmation continuously without leaving any spaces between the words)

"Iradiatepositivityandconfidencewherev erigo"

_____

_____

_____

_____

_____

_____

_____

_____

_____

_____

_____

_____

_____

_____

_____

_____

_____

_____

_____

Journal Question.

Do you feel that your self-esteem and confidence has increased since starting this journal, if so in what way?

Affirmation # 88

(Complete and repeat the affirmation)

Today I will feel good about myself all day because

_____

_____

_____

_____

_____

_____

_____

_____

_____

_____

_____

_____

_____

_____

_____

_____

_____

Journal Question.

How was your day?

Affirmation # 89

(Decorate this page with some love)

"Every day I grow in the capacity to love myself"

Journal entry.

There have been several affirmations that refer to loving yourself, do you feel more comfortable saying this affirmation and do you feel that you have a greater capacity to love yourself?

Affirmation # 90

(Repeat and complete this affirmation)

I believe in myself because_____

Journal Question.

Explore this affirmation further.

Affirmation # 91

(Complete and repeat this affirmation)

When I see myself in the future I am -

_____

_____

_____

_____

_____

_____

_____

_____

_____

_____

_____

_____

_____

_____

_____

_____

_____

_____

Journal entry.

Make a list of goals for the future -

Affirmation # 92

(Repeat the affirmation 10 times before writing it. Don't forget to add a border)

"I accept what I cannot change and change what I can"

Journal Question.

What things do you need to accept and what things have you got the power to change?

Affirmation # 93

(Repeat 10 times then rewrite)

"I recognise that I am a valuable worthy person"

Journal Entry.

Do you recognise your own worth or is that difficult for you? What do you need to do, or what beliefs do you need to develop in order to accept that you are worthy?

Affirmation # 94

"I am responsible for creating my self-esteem and I am going to stand tall and walk with pride"

Journal entry.

★

"TODAY AND EVERY DAY I WAKE UP WITH A POSITIVE MIND, A HEART FULL OF LOVE AND JOY IN MY SOUL. WITH THESE THREE GIFTS MY LIFE IS ALREADY COMPLETE"

Journal Question.

How do you feel your attitude has changed, what things do you think and feel differently about?

Affirmation # 96

(Go crazy and draw a random pattern on the page over the lines and then colour it before you write the affirmations)

"Today I celebrate my independence, freedom and ability to make choices & I choose to value and enjoy the good things in my life"

Journal Question.

What things do you value most in your life?

_____

_____

_____

_____

_____

_____

_____

_____

_____

_____

_____

_____

_____

_____

_____

_____

_____

_____

_____

_____

_____

_____

Affirmation # 97

(Repeat this affirmation out loud and write NO as many times as you can on the page) maybe colour in all the letter O's

"I have the strength and courage to stand up for myself and I can say NO when I need to"

Journal Question.

What things do you need to say NO to but currently find difficult?
Also, are there certain people that you find difficult to say NO to,
and if so why is it so hard?

Affirmation # 98

I accept myself for who I am without fear of rejection from others.

_____

_____

_____

_____

_____

_____

_____

_____

_____

_____

_____

_____

_____

_____

_____

_____

_____

_____

_____

_____

Journal Question.

What is your greatest fear about being rejected?

Affirmation # 99

(Keep repeating the affirmation while you write it out)

"I expect the best. I accept the best, I deserve the best that's because I am the BEST"

_____

_____

_____

_____

_____

_____

_____

_____

_____

_____

_____

_____

_____

_____

_____

_____

_____

_____

Journal entry.

I deserve the best because_____

_____
_____
_____
_____
_____
_____
_____
_____
_____
_____
_____
_____
_____
_____
_____
_____
_____
_____
_____
_____

Never forget that you deserve the best because you are the best. That's right. You are the best.

Affirmation # 100

"Every day my self-esteem strengthens and grows and I feel AMAZING"

Journal entry.

Complete this letter – Dear Self-esteem, Thank you for _____

_____

_____

_____

_____

_____

_____

_____

_____

_____

_____

_____

_____

_____

_____

_____

_____

_____

_____

_____

_____

Affirmation # 101

(Decorate this page using lots of patterns and colours)

I am **beautiful** and talented.

I am caring and **courageous.**

I am **loving** and loveable.

I am strong and determined.

I am **honest** and sincere and

Overall I am a **wonderful**

human being.

*

Journal entry.

Congratulations on completing this workbook. I'm sure it has taken a lot of dedication and hard work on your part and I hope that you enjoyed it as well. Now for the final Journal Question.

In what ways have you changed since you started the workbook?.

_____

_____

_____

_____

_____

_____

_____

_____

_____

_____

_____

_____

_____

_____

_____

_____

_____

*

Make a list of your favourite affirmations below.

*

What do you think you have learnt about yourself during this process?

*

What has been the hardest part of completing this journal?

What has been the best part of working through this journal?

Also by

Tony T Robinson.

*

The Happiness Journal.

*

My 365 Day Guided Journal.

*

101 Journal questions for women.

*

101 Self Discovery Journal Prompts.

*

101 Quick and Easy Confidence Quotes.

*

101 Confidence Quotes that will change your life.

*

101 "I AM" Power Affirmations.

*

Made in the USA
Las Vegas, NV
15 June 2022

50252570R00134